Amoy A. Laurence

A Quick & Easy Guide to Help You Transition from Woman to Wife

ISBN: 978-976-96398-8-1

Cover images by Christopher James (CJam Photos).
Cover design by Christopher Lawrence (Logomeplease).
Proofread by Shanna Monteith

Printed on Demand

First printing edition 2021.

Anointed Writers Publishing
anointedwriterspublishing@gmail.com

Website: www.theanointedwriter.com/awpublishing

ALSO BY AMOY A. LAWRENCE

31 Days of Affirmations
for Teenage Girls & Young Adult Women

WOMAN OR WIFE

↔

Amoy A. Lawrence

Dedication

This book is dedicated to **all the women who are on their journey from woman to wife.** Who you are as you develop in your womanhood, will later affect how you function as a wife. How you transition from one phase into the next is up to you and the route you choose to take.

To my GIFTED GEMS, I love you unconditionally. You came into my life when I needed sound Christian sisterhood and you delivered just that. Thank you for the laughs, the rebukes and the circle of trust. May your storehouses never be empty and may you continue to serve the Lord with gladness.

To my mother, you've taught me survival and what to never accept as love from a man. You showed me what it means to be a strong, praying woman. Your life is full of purpose and meaning and I vow to help you live out the years God has restored unto you.

Contents

Foreword

Written by: Prophet Shambraé K. Gamble

Throughout the years, women have been fed many perspectives and views on what it means to fully walk in their role as well as fully assume their purpose in the earth. Mrs. Amoy A. Lawrence has taken on the task through this incredibly insightful book to give women all over the world a concise and clear distinction of what it means to fully walk in the world of womanhood as well as transition into the role of a wife.

Womanhood has suffered many false and one-sided definitions that have limited women around the world from tapping into their full God-given potential. In our modern society, womanhood has been confined to vanity, competition, and sexual liberation. If you survey different movements, being a woman is no different than being female. This could not be further from the truth. When God built the woman from the remnants of the man, he built a functional entity with unique capabilities, desires, and capacity. Womanhood supersedes simply belonging to the female species, it encompasses the ability to improve and increase whatever is planted within, whether it be a generation, an idea, a dream, or a calling. The spiritual force that is womanhood incubates the plans and purposes of God and converts them into reality. No wonder, that the Word could only become flesh through the canals of a woman. A woman's essence is the carrier and materializer of whatever God desires to do in the earth. Until we as women understand the power within, we will continue to devalue ourselves as insufficient and inferior. The woman is the crowned jewel of God's creation. She is the fully unique, original idea of the Master. She is the full expression and beauty of God's creative prowess. She carries her Father's creative DNA. The strength and power within the woman to conquer, carry, and create is unmatched and irreplaceable.

Womanhood is a discipline, and due to the depreciation of women power over the years, womanhood must also be taught and re-taught. Young girls in today's society are maturing physically, but are stunted in their spiritual development. This creates a by-product of dysfunction that blinds women from seeing their true potential and purpose. Subsequently, most women are spiritually and emotionally unprepared for marriage. The scriptures give us various examples and apparatus for what the godly wife looks like. Many girls pursue this biblical ideal without learning the essence of womanhood and thus find themselves aspiring to a man and a wedding that they do not have the spiritual capacity to handle or sustain. A woman who is secure in her womanhood is just as essential to a man's vision as a man who is secure in his manhood is to a woman's security. Until a woman has mastered herself as a woman, she will never understand herself as a wife. In a world where divorces in the church are at an all-time high, this truth is a culture shifting phenomenon that is crucial for the future of Christian marriages.

Amoy is dear to my heart, she is a fiery ball of compassion, wit, and intellectual prowess. I have watched her mature into a woman drenched in class, poise, and raw power. She and her husband Christopher are two of the purest people I have met in my lifetime. I love them with all of my heart. I am fully confident in her ability to walk you through a comprehensive understanding of your evolution from woman to wife. Giving you scripturally sound strategies and testimonies that will challenge, convict, and change you. It is my distinct honour and pleasure to welcome you into this spiritual incubator that is guaranteed to shift your thinking and change your life.

Introduction
Woman or Wife

Then I heard the Lord say:

When God is preparing you to step into the role of a godly wife there are certain characteristics that you must develop. You must:

- Pray
- Know the Word, have a desire for the Word and read the Word.
- Know how to activate favour by submitting to the Lord's call and will for your life by walking in faith and obedience.
- Learn to communicate with the simple yet complex mind of a man.
- Be able to see beyond what you see in the natural.
- Understand submission to God. **(See John 3:30)**
- Be patient
- Be loyal
- Be welcoming
- Be trusted
- Be whole

- Be pure in heart, body and spirit
- Be industrious
- Be productive
- Be wise (financially)
- Be selfless
- Be compassionate
- Boldly represent your husband and protect his reputation
- Be honourable
- Live a life that communicates nobility
- Fear the Lord

God has been speaking to me about the true intent for godly relationships and the foundation of godly marriages. He says our thought processes and actions have been affected by generational mishaps in culture, society and homes. The breakdown has unleashed confusion in sexual identity, an attack on the reproductive health of women, the birth of non-biblical women empowerment ideologies, and a rise in nonchalance and disregard for establishing strong family units. Women and men have become scarred and hurt. Men have become careless with the responsibilities attached to sexual intercourse. Women have become fearful of intimate relationships with men because of the non-existence and/or breakdowns in father-daughter relationships.

We understand that these challenges and responsibilities don't only rest on the woman. However, this book is for the woman. The woman who is desirous of becoming a wife and called to become one. We are living in a time where we realise that emphasis has always been placed on the woman to be worthy of marriage. Women are now calling men to a higher standard and are requesting more than the bare minimum requirement that society has placed on them. The women expect godly character, friendship, high standards of love and more. It is understood that responsibility is not only to be placed on the woman and that men should be just as intentional about their development into manhood. Later, you will read from JaQuan X. Gamble's perspective on what is required of a godly man who is called to love a godly woman in a godly marriage.

As for the women, we start with you and focus on you for the purpose of this book. Retrain the mind and spirit. Return to the godly principles surrounding dating with the premise that relationships should aim for marriage. Your body is a temple so treat it holy; let not your preferences influenced by unrealistic expectations, heart protection (emotional walls), hurt and bitterness override God's true intent and purposes for marriage. Marriage – when done God's way – is a selfless pursuit to please God that stretches you to become the marriage model God wants to use as influence for the next generation.

Will you submit? Will you answer the call? Are you Woman or Wife?

Join in re-establishing God's truth in relationships and marriages.

Follow the Movement on social media

@theanointedwriter
#WomanOrWife #TheAnointedWriter

CHAPTER 1

The Holy Order of Woman

Eve was a woman with a holy order. She was placed on the earth to be her husband's help meet. Genesis 2:18 - ***And the Lord God said, it is not good that the man should be alone; I will make him a help meet for him.*** God had vision and purpose for her to be a friend, companion and lover to her husband – Adam. God had great tasks for Adam in the garden of Eden. He was the 'Man of the Garden' and everything was in his care. The story unfolds and God has one instruction for Adam: do not eat from the tree of knowledge of good and evil **(Genesis 2:16-17).** God then provides Adam with a wife and it is assumed that he passed on the instruction to her as 'Man of the Garden'. In summary, the enemy seduced the woman to eat from the tree of knowledge of good and evil which led the two to be exiled from the garden. Adam named his wife Eve to mean life spring and life giver, because she was the mother of all the living. Eve had a holy order and like Eve – the foundation of womanhood – women were created with a holy order.

A holy order is a divine purpose, mandate and instruction from God to aid in the advancement of the Kingdom. It is who you are, what you are created to do, and how you are destined to do it. There are a few points to note from the creation, fall, and life of Eve.

Eve was:

- Created to **support** her husband **(Genesis 2:18).** It is important to know that as women we are designed to support the men in carrying out their God-given assignments.

- A **companion**. God said that it was not good for Adam to be alone. He needed a friend, a confidant, and a companion.

- Bone of Adam's bone and flesh of his flesh **(Genesis 2:23)**. Eve was a part of him; she was **spiritually connected**. This gave room for great influence over her husband. He trusted her and listened to her. Whatever she did affected him and whatever he did affected her. They were required to be in unison flowing with the grace that flows from one to the other.

- The **entry point of attack** which led to the fall. She was the point of attack; the one who could be influenced and easily deceived. **(Genesis 3).** In many societies, though the man leads the family, the woman is considered to be the neck and backbone of the family unit. She is the one possessing the intuition, the favour, and the spiritual insight that affords her the ability to aid in the sound decisions made when leading the family. **Proverbs 31** describes a wife of noble character, "She is clothed with strength and dignity, and she laughs without fear of the future. When she speaks, her words are wise, and she gives instructions with kindness. She carefully watches everything in her household and suffers nothing from laziness.

- Full of **vision** and curiosity for **insight (Genesis 3:6)**. I consider these to be few of the many characteristics of a creative which alludes to her being life giver and the mother of all creation.

- **Submitted. (Genesis 3:16)** - … ***and thy desire shall be to thy husband, and he shall rule over thee.***

- **The mother of spiritual warfare. (Genesis 3:15)** - ***And I will put enmity between thee and the woman, and between thy seed and her seed; it shall bruise thy head, and thou shalt bruise his heel.*** The woman is always at odds with the devil. I believe she is the first to see his dirty tricks (woman intuition?) and in the same breath she is always under attack. She is fighting to never to be tricked again.

Women are called to the man to be supporters, companions, connected, vulnerable, creative visionaries, submitted and prayerful. The holy order of the woman encompasses all these and more. As you explore the transition from woman to wife, prepare your heart to be transformed and your spirit to be enlightened.

NOTES

CHAPTER 2

The Definition of Woman

Exploring the biblical basis of womanhood leads to a cultural analysis of who woman is. The definition of woman has seen much transformation as time progressed. In the days of the bible, woman spanned from the lower class to the middle class to royalty. Woman still fits all these positions and more. However, one thing that has changed and is changing is the culture. Womanhood is represented differently across cultures and with the surge of social media influence, cross-cultural impact is more evident.

The definitions of woman and womanhood are very vague according to books and dictionaries. They say that womanhood is the state of being a woman and the word woman is defined as an adult human female. What? That's it? The value of woman and her strength cannot be limited to such simple definitions. There's so much more to being a woman.

Womanhood is evident in the tears women cry for their families. It is living in the prayers of the mothers. Womanhood is defined by the women who have overcome rape and domestic abuse. Womanhood encompasses hopes, fears, dreams, failures, visions and aspirations. It is wrapped in the firsts – the first woman Prime Minister of Jamaica or the first African American Woman Vice President of the United States. It is not one dimensional neither fully positive nor negative; it is well rounded, diverse and dynamic. The definition of woman is best defined by woman herself. Let's explore what the women have to say about womanhood or being a woman.

Jameka Anderson

"Being a woman requires too many dispositions at times, if I can be honest. I believe that women have often been categorized to have to be one specific way which originates from patriarchal points of view. If we are direct or passionate, we are told to soften up. If we show that nurturing side, we are told to toughen up. Society will toss you from the east to the west in your identity as a woman if you let it. I've fallen into this trap so many different times. I've compared myself to others which robbed me of the view to see myself how God designed me. On my journey to true womanhood through the eyes of ABBA, I'm constantly learning and unlearning what it means to be a woman. We are called to, but not limited to being God-fearing and hard workers **(Proverbs 31),** keepers of the home **(Titus 2:5),** and we are led to focus on the beauty that comes from the Holy Spirit versus our outer appearance **(1 Peter 3:4)**. He created us with supernatural depth. God has created women with a different type of strength, emotionally and physically. And I also know [now] that God didn't create us solely to become wives and mothers or only to cater to the needs of others. He has us here for a purpose. He decided to create me to first and foremost bring Him glory, and to lead others to get to know Him so that they can do the same. These are just a few reasons why women are here, but there is so much more. I'll continue to learn as God teaches me individually, as well as in the community of other great women."

Candace Sorrell

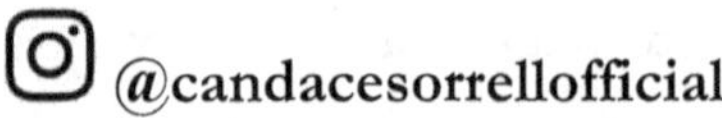

"To me, being a woman is beauty in itself. Her strength, poise, determination and willpower to see a task through is remarkable. She stands in confidence knowing that she is worth more than what others see. She doesn't respond to mishaps inappropriately but with great elegance. Her DNA is the makeup and representation of Christ and she leads in that same grace. A real woman's love has no condition to it and selfless in every way. She stands her ground and changes the world by doing so."

Davia Thomas

"Though a woman is almost always associated with being a mother and a wife, being a woman entails more than just that. We are equally created in the image and likeness of God, just as the man is. Being a woman entails innately loving, nurturing and making sacrifices for the betterment of those around her. Consider the widow of Zarephath who gave of her very last bread to feed the Prophet, Elijah. Not only did she feed him, but she also provided a place for him to stay. Women are tender-hearted, yet their mental strength is second to none. Womanhood is synonymous to being a visionary. If you share an idea or concept with a woman, you will witness that concept come to life."

Shanna Monteith

@sha_nnerr

"Sure. No prob!" was my immediate response to Amoy's request to share my thoughts on what it means to be a woman. I mean, I'm a woman and have been for years, and as we know, experience is the best teacher so explaining this would be a walk in the park, right? WRONG. My first attempt at answering the question sent me straight to Google, which is a reflex of mine whenever tasked with defining things.

"Ok Google. What does it mean to be a woman?"

"Here are the top search results:

1. "I think being female means you're strong, capable, worthy, and vulnerable…"- Seventeen
2. "When this question first popped into my head, I Googled it like a good Generation Y-er. The results were less than disappointing…" -HuffPost

3. "It means wearing make-up, high heels and skinny dresses that are glued to a nice skinny body…"- Medium
4. "Being a woman means far too many things to put into words…" – Odyssey

...and the search results went on…

Obviously, like me, Google was struggling with the definition and so I was left on my own, with my personal experiences (which suddenly felt so limited) to wing it. This is what I came up with…

One would think that having breasts, a vagina and ovaries would be an adequate response to the question of what it means to be a woman. Apparently, it isn't enough. In my estimation, being a woman takes on different definitions based on the circumstance. When you think of a woman as a mother you think of a protective or defensive, patient, overly understanding being whose weakness lies in the very thing she fights to be strong for, her children. Woman as a wife - reverend, faithful, virtuous and most importantly (and highly overlooked) subservient…submissive 'to a fault.' Put that same 'woman' in a nuclear family structure (wife + mother) and she becomes a thread, one that so aptly weaves the fabrics of a household together despite the incompatibility of each fibre. Then there's the woman as a sole entity. She is daring, strong-willed, wild and uncontrollable - a force which shamelessly and deceptively destroys everything in her path to ensure self is satisfied, despite the damage. With an innate ability to survive, the woman has little to no regard for others.

Shavonne Mateen

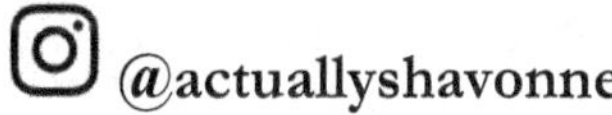

Womanhood to me first begins with identity in God; knowing who you are and what you stand for. Standing firm on the fact that before any other title I'm called to, I'm God's daughter. There comes dignity in that. From dignity, strength, grace, and power begin to flow. Even as life is always changing, remembering your posture as a daughter fuels a woman to go after purpose, adjust to any circumstance, and walk in the fullness of destiny.

Womanhood often transitions as life progresses. As women step into roles in families, careers, friendships, and even day to day personal evolving, each component presents another opportunity to embrace a new side to ourselves. That same sense and acceptance of identity grows deeper. So, womanhood is transcendent. It is the essence of wisdom, exudes light, epitomizing the honourable, and is edifying to the environment for which a woman adapts.

As I am personally transitioning from teenager to woman, I'm learning that at every turn of life, there's required consistency. Because of the constant change women go through, there's always a need to reset yourself in your identity. I wasn't the same woman at twenty that I'm evolving into at twenty-one. So, I have to ask myself: what are my passions? What has changed about how I see myself? What relationships do I have now? Where have I grown and where do I now lack? I'm finding all of these questions are necessary to ask yourself. This is how we adapt. Womanhood is a full cycle of growth, self-evaluation, identity of self, and it is what gives a woman strength and distinction.

Paula-Kaye Murphy

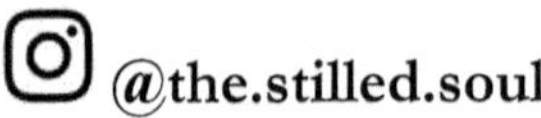

When I consider what womanhood means to me, my mind goes to the complexities that accompany being a woman. The moods, the emotions, the thought patterns, the life experiences that impact me -

everything. I consider all of that and my initial thought is "womanhood is learning how to master these complexities". The more I process it, the more I realize that my complexities aren't something to master in the sense of trying to control and rein them in. They are, instead, qualities I should learn to be at peace with. By being at peace with these complexities, I can understand even more why I am the way I am and how my experiences have contributed to who I am developing into as a woman.

Being a woman means navigating different aspects of you that are sometimes on opposing ends of the spectrum. It means being both gentle and strong. It means being vulnerable yet resilient. It is being assertive as well as submissive and being open to new experiences while holding true to your core self. Learning to find a balance between these opposites has helped me to step into roles and spaces that I otherwise would have struggled to thrive in. Granted, it's taken me a while to understand my womanhood and there is a lot more uncovering, understanding and growing to do. But for all that it is, womanhood for me is blossoming.

To make sense of it all - being a woman, in my estimation, means existing as a shapeless entity with the ***ability*** to find form in whatever situation she is thrown. Woman, in all her forms, I believe, is powerful beyond measure, with how she chooses to use such power being the key driver of the aforementioned 'ability'."

Include your own definition in your notes below or email it to the author at anointedwriterspublishing@gmail.com to be featured on social media.

NOTES

CHAPTER 3

Woman – The Accelerator

Chemistry teaches the function of the catalyst which is a substance that initiates or accelerates a chemical reaction without itself being consumed. For example, if you add vinegar to baking soda, a chemical reaction occurs. The vinegar acts as the catalyst to initiate the reaction or increase the rate of the reaction. When a catalyst is added to a reactive substance, the presence of that catalyst causes the reaction to occur. The more you add, the greater the reaction.

Have you ever thought of yourself as a catalyst or an accelerator? Someone who initiates change or speeds up the rate of change? Think of the verse Proverbs 18:22 which says ***"The man who finds a wife finds a treasure, and he receives favour from the Lord."*** God gave me the most amazing revelation about the woman being referred to in this scripture. He said, "Woman, you are a catalyst, an accelerator, and an agent of change. Your presence causes things to happen speedily but you are not affected in the process. Your husband awaits your strength and favour. You are his activation and you propel him into purpose. Your patience is vital and your preparation is necessary."

I pray that that nugget made you as excited as I was when I first received it. I continue to feel excitement whenever I repeat it. Ladies, you are the prize and you should never forget it. A man should be pursuing purpose in his individual spiritual journey but think of what happens when the purpose accelerator comes along. You make things happen! Men across the globe have expressed how much their lives change when they meet their spouse. With your power packed identity, you can help him move from Carpenter to CEO of The Carpenter's Factory and Warehouse. The man will obtain the favour of the Lord when he finds a wife but you must be willing to help.

I find that many women today think only of themselves and what they can receive from a relationship when there is so much power in what they offer. I don't think women truly understand the power they possess. Your ability to see beyond the physical and speak to the purpose in a man is not an ability to take lightly. Woman, you were designed to accelerate and ignite change.

Here's what you need to know about your acceleration ability:

- Favour calls the husband's life into alignment. Proverbs 18:22 - ***"The man who finds a wife finds a treasure, and he receives favour from the Lord."***

- You're his destiny helper by default. Destiny helpers are individuals sent along our paths here on earth in times of great need to propel God's people into their God-given purpose. There are usually earthly obstacles trying to prevent persons from walking into their destiny. As a destiny helper, God has blessed you with opportunities, influence and strategies to help his servants along their purpose paths.

- You are his earthly guide. You serve as a voice of reason. It is important for the woman to know who she is and the role she plays in a man's life. Being able to trust your instincts and decisions is equally as important. Each female is born with an innate quality known as female intuition. Intuition is one of the woman's many superpowers. As a woman on a journey to becoming a wife, intuition never becomes irrelevant. In fact, you need it now more than ever. Men are logical beings while women are more intuitive. This balance is no mistake and your intuition is a necessary quality to have. Where men see logic only, the woman's intuition is needed to ensure that the logic – when implemented- is beneficial to both parties.

NOTES

CHAPTER 4

What Help?

In Genesis 2:18 God said, **"It is not good for the man to be alone. I will make a helper who is just right for him."** Most women can admit that they don't pay attention to that word 'helper' or 'helpmeet'- in other translations. They know that it is not good for the man to be alone and God will make someone who is 'right' for him. However, most women think that the word helper paints the picture of a woman who has abandoned her own life to be dedicated to a man and, is seen as less than the man. That is not the case at all.

I believe the idea stems from a time when women were seen as the inferior gender in society. In the Industrial Age, women had to work in factories and mines to help pay for their family's cost of living and they weren't as valued as the men in the workplace. Since as far back as colonization, black women, in particular, have formed involuntary, destructive habits of giving of themselves to the detriment of their mental, physical and emotional well-being. Whether it was for surviving the workplace or for the betterment of their families, for decades women have stripped themselves of their own dreams and desires for the betterment of others. All without realizing the lasting influences their actions will have on the generations to come.

Although these periods have ended, the residue remains in society today and women want no more of it. The man they marry must be able to wine, dine and provide for them with no added stress. Women want to be able to pursue careers, be powerful women in society and celebrated equally without having to sacrifice value in marriage.

In my estimation, the area that has been most affected by the remnant of these industrial ideologies is marriage. In many homes, a healthy family sees the woman giving up the ability to go to work and earn to stay home and take care of the family. And, even if the woman does work, she is expected to function in minimal roles while continuing to maintain the home.

During this time, the man also works but oftentimes has no obligations to the home outside of his provision. In addition to that, while the woman is selflessly sacrificing her time and energy for her family, the intimacy in her marriage suffers and as a result, the man searches for that intimacy in the bosom of other women.

It sounds like a movie but this is the reality of many marriages. Women who were raised in environments with marriages of this nature, have grown to understand the reality of what they were witnessing. They now understand that the seeming functionality that they viewed being displayed was often a mask layer covering deeper issues. And, to avoid following along the path of those gone before them, many of these women have concluded that marriage is not all that it cracks up to be. They have concluded that the role of the wife is nothing to desire. For others, they have made internal vows never to be the selfless, sacrificing wives they were raised emulating. They don't want 40 years of seemingly functional marriage filled with negligence and infidelity. Instead, they must work to empower themselves, gain independence, and not depend on a man to provide for them.

These realities have birthed an interesting phenomenon in society. We can now see where it is more popular to be selfish than it is to be selfless, especially in relationships. ***'Feminist', 'Women Empowerment', 'The Rise of the Woman.', and others*** are all terms we hear in the modern society. Not that women have not been on the journey to rise above the hardships they've faced, but you can say that we are at an all-time high. The word feminism is the buzz word/movement of the century. ***Equal rights and justice for all women*** is at the forefront of the women empowerment agenda in most spaces. This is great – especially for the black woman - but I am afraid that many are getting carried away by the euphoria of the liberation they experience. For many women, women empowerment is quickly becoming ***male refusal.*** And instead of healing the wounds the women before us have left on our psyche, we've moved into the culture of declaring that men are trash, men are worthless and simply not doing enough to match the achievements of women.

Helpmeet
(Heb. 'ezer ke-negdo; i.e., "a help as his counterpart" = a help suitable to him), a wife (Genesis 2:18-20).

What most women fail to realize is that, biblically, the woman is created for the man to be his submitted equal to carry out purpose on earth and to advance the Kingdom. Submitted equal? It's quite the paradox, I know, but that is really what it is. Remember, the scripture says, **"It is not good for man to be alone; I will make a helper who is just right for him."** Woman, your role is clearly a deliberate inclusion in God's creation process. Think of all the things Adam had to do in the garden of Eden, as he was given dominion over God's creations. With all the mental and physical strain from such great responsibility, it is no wonder that God needed to create a companion for him.

As a woman, it is not your duty to resent the call, but to find out what your role entails as his helper without neglecting your own development. Each man's help is unique to him so no two helpers will function the same. However, each helper should possess the fundamental qualities that are submission, partnership and teamwork. Later, we will delve into what makes a man worthy to be submitted to. I can see you rolling your eyes and scoffing at the thought of submitting to some of these men in the dating pool. I will never set you up to be of service to a man who will be incapable of watering your own development. Being a helpmeet seems like an unfair game when you isolate the role. Remember, it is a trusting partnership designed to advance the Kingdom. It requires two capable individuals coming together for the greater good of the Kingdom.

NOTES

CHAPTER 5

Understanding Submission

Submission has become a curse word for many Christian, single women who weren't exposed to healthy examples of submission or correct teachings on the topic. It isn't common to think of submission as a holy act in marriage. Oftentimes women see submission as punishment, being stripped of any power and a slave/slave owner type dynamic. In fact, submission is designed by God to facilitate a structured flow and representation of His spirit in the family. Paul in **Ephesians 5:28-30** tells the husband to love his wife as he loves his own body and equates the husband's care of his wife with that of Christ's for His church.

The loving husband submits his will to God and takes instruction from Him for the affairs of the family. In this context, the wife willingly submits to her husband.

godly submission in a marriage brings unison and peace. Unfortunately, many of the future wives of today have witnessed a breakdown in society at large and sadly in Christian marriages as well. When women fail to choose godly men, submit to God's process and refuse to submit to the godly men they've been given, the biblical standard suffers.

As a woman who aspires to be a wife and is well on your way, you can commit to breaking the cycle by learning and implementing the biblical standard of marriage. There are what I call the Ss of submission that will help you better understand what it takes to be a truly submitted wife. Many who rebel against the biblical standard of submission in a marriage have no understanding or experience with the following concepts. So, let's explore:

Strength

Isaiah 41:10 - So do not fear, for I am with you; do not be dismayed, for I am your God. I will strengthen you and help you; I will uphold you with my righteous right hand.

Psalm 46:1-3 - God is our refuge and strength, an ever-present help in trouble. Therefore, we will not fear, though the earth gives way and the mountains fall into the heart of the sea, though its waters roar and foam and the mountains quake with their surging.

1 Chronicles 16:11 - Seek the LORD and his strength; seek his presence continually!

Have you ever truly had to rely on God's strength? You know, being at a place of spiritual and physical weakness. There's no strength to move, no strength to pray; it's as if you are paralyzed and the storms of life are raging, as the Christian cliché puts it. You have no money, no hope, and no one to turn to so you give it all to God. It is in that moment that you will realize what it truly means to cast your cares on Jesus and gain His strength.

Servitude

If you're free-spirited you won't fully understand servitude, mainly because servitude means you have to answer to a master, like a servant does. For many, servitude is likened to slavery. I mean, by definition, servitude is a brutal form of slavery. If you look at the term in the natural sense, you will want nothing to do with it. However, if you assess the word in the spiritual, you will realize that it is one of the key characteristics that God requires of us. He wants us to have a heart of selfless service towards Him and others.

In the context of preparing for marriage and submitting to a husband, it is important to have a heart of servitude. One of the revelations God gave to me recently is that the wife's service to her husband unlocks divine favour that will benefit them both throughout their marriage. **Proverbs 18:22** states that whoso findeth a wife findeth a good thing, and obtaineth favour of the Lord. In the finding, an initial favour is unlocked. However, that favour regenerates and multiplies as the wife serves her husband throughout their marriage. Take Ruth for example. Ruth personifies service in my opinion. She had a heart for service in her waiting and preparation for her husband to be and I believe she continued serving him all the days of their marriage. Her service unlocked divine favour for her and her family.

This is how I want you to think of servitude in the context of submission. As a woman preparing to marry, learn to develop an attitude of servitude that will fuel the favour in your marriage. Make it one of your duties as a wife to serve your husband. Ensure that his emotional needs are met and ensure that you do your part to cultivate a space of rest for him. While men are called to protect and provide for us, as wives it should be our duty to ensure that he can find rest in us. One way to do that is through serving him.

Solace

Solace. Say it with me. So…lace. The word alone is calming and soothing don't you agree? To give solace to someone is to provide a place of comfort or consolation in a time of great distress or sadness. Solace. If you should do an assessment of your current mannerisms, attitudes, how you deal with distress or how you face sadness; would you say that you are able to give solace to someone else?

I was hinting at this 'S' of submission as I wrote about servitude. I want women to understand that despite the societal depictions of women in relationships, we can't assume the role of the nagging wife. Men process things differently and I'm sure we can all agree to that. TD Jakes mentioned in his sermon titled 'Model Homes' that a man can mentally or psychologically leave a relationship without physically leaving. This usually happens when the woman is being a nag. You know, when she has to get her point across at all times. Even to the extent where he has stopped responding but she continues. According to Bishop Jakes, silence almost never means that you've won the argument. Silence means that he has checked out and left you alone. He went on to mention that when a man is at this point it is the hardest task for him to return to you emotionally. Why? Because he doesn't feel safe. So, how do you – as a woman – cultivate an attitude of solace or give solace to a man in distress or sadness? Be his peace. Sounds cliché, right? You've heard this so many times in popular culture, "be his peace.". Please note that a man who has not found his own peace cannot receive peace from a woman. My definition for peace in this sense is a non-toxic environment that promotes clear, effective communication geared towards problem solving as opposed to problem igniting. In this space, emotional needs are met, respect and honour are maintained, and both walk away at peace and more empowered than ever before.

Synergy & Support

In my opinion, one of the scriptures that bring to the fore the synergy and support necessary in marriage is **Ecclesiastes 4:9-12** which says "Two are better than one; because they have a good reward for their labour. For if they fall, the one will lift up his fellow: but woe to him that is alone when he falleth; for he hath not another to help him up. Again, if two lie together, then they have heat: but how can one be warm alone? And if one prevails against him, two shall withstand him; and a threefold cord is not quickly broken." This scripture highlights the effectiveness of the synergy and support between married couples with God at the centre.

In order to grasp the necessity of submission, one must understand what it means to submit to God, authority and the process of walking in obedience to fulfil the will of God for your life. Many times, as Christians, we believe in our own strength, abilities, and emotions more than the sovereignty of God. As a result, we attend church and acknowledge God but we fail to develop a submitted relationship with Him. When preparing for marriage, it is imperative that you cultivate that relationship and walk in obedience with the Word. It won't make the wait any easier but it will make it clearer and more purposeful. Submit to God and submit to the process so that ultimately you will be able to submit to your husband.

NOTES

CHAPTER 6

Tools for the Wait

Whether you've been waiting for a long time or a little while, the wait is the most integral part of the transition process from woman to wife. In the wait we are challenged; in the wait we are refined. The wait is there to help you develop and prepare for the marriage that is to come. It is important to apply the necessary tools to help you transition smoothly.

Even as I pen this chapter, I can see a woman looking at how hard the wait is and asking herself if marriage is for her. Yes, marriage is for anyone who wants it and is willing to submit to

God's process and conditioning. I personally don't subscribe to the idea that individuals are called to a life of singleness. It is a notion drenched in fear and doubt that is not from God. There may be instances where, based on the assignment God has given to you, marriage may not be an ideal choice. However, in those rare instances, I believe God will communicate clearly if that is the path, He would have you walk.

The wait may be challenging for many reasons. Each woman has her own struggle during the waiting period. Some find it hard to abstain from sex and maintain purity, others grow impatient or lose hope in love and many cry that there are no good men left. Whatever your struggle may be, understand that as long as there is love for God and faith in Him, there is hope. With the right tools you can wait faithfully and patiently on the one God has created for you.

It's funny how I am writing to you about waiting, as I am currently on day 6 of my 10-day isolation due to COVID-19 in a foreign country approximately 1,448 miles away from my husband. I know right? From this point of view, I can tell you that waiting is HARD. Being away from something you really want and desire but not being able to grasp it is almost defeating. I can just imagine how it is with waiting for marriage.

You see those around you finding love, being asked the question and walking down the aisle. As hard as it is, let me help you to navigate this time.

In my own season of waiting, I learned the importance of maintaining a relationship with God. God spent time teaching me what I needed to know in preparation for the next season which was meeting my potential spouse and getting ready for marriage. And, that's the tool I want to give you:

Cultivate a relationship with God that is strong in faith, trust and obedience. From there, you will receive clarity, direction and instruction. In your wait, it is as important as it is necessary to cultivate a relationship with God and strengthen the discipline to maintain it. I always emphasize that each woman's journey to the altar is unique and even her life thereafter. The only way we can truly know if we are on the right path, is to let the one who is in control of our destinies lead us; and that is Jehovah. He is all knowing and all powerful. If **Luke 12:7** tells us in the Word that even the very hairs on our head are numbered and we are of more value than many sparrows, then I believe it is safe to assume that God would care about every single area of our lives including who we marry.

I share the story often about how God led me to pray daily for my future spouse who I hadn't met yet at the time. I was in a period where I was growing frustrated in the wait. God promised me a spouse so why was it taking so long? You can be modest all you want but being single bites! Not in a way that is agonizing and filled with disdain for the season, but in a way that is unnecessarily challenging as it relates to wants and desires. For those of you who weren't born and raised in the church and are not saints, I feel your pain. You've tasted and you have seen, so denying yourself of those pleasures is a challenge in and of itself. So yes, I was growing frustrated. Having gone through the disappointment and heartbreak of having to let go of a 'situationship' I thought was heading to marriage; God said it was time to pray and allow Him to lead me to the one He kept for me. The day I started praying was the day the ball started rolling and my eyes began to open.

Before I go into the specific steps of praying for your future spouse, I want you to know that not every woman is ready for marriage and that is okay. Don't be pressured by your age or society's expectations of you. The MARRIAGE is far more important than the wedding so walk slowly and carefully to the altar. Grab your notebook of choice, get a pen and read on.

Step 1 – Pre-Prayer

I call Step 1 the preparation step. Please note that the moment you begin to actively pray for your future spouse, you are activating and setting the ball in motion. So, before you begin to actively pray for your future spouse, do a self-check. Ask yourself these questions:

- How is my relationship with God?
- What is my purpose?
- Do I value a relationship more than the will of God for my life?
- Am I functioning in the will of God?
- Am I whole? (e.g., Healed from past emotional hurts)
- Am I free? (e.g., from soul ties and emotional baggage)
- Am I confident?

Once issues are present, actively work with God as your guide and therapy if you must, on being the best you. Many persons misunderstand this stage. They believe that they are on the journey to being the perfect woman for the man. When, in fact, the woman is being the best version of herself in order to glorify and honour God through her relationship.

Step 2 – The LIST

Step 2 is very important. This is where you start to practically see the necessity of the relationship you've been cultivating with God. You must be submitted to Him and able to trust His guidance and directives. Many women often overthink the idea of developing a relationship with God. I assume that most – if not all - of you reading this are Christians and understand the foundations of prayer and the Word. That's all you really need to begin. Dedicate time to praying and reading the Word of God. In your moments dedicated to Him, you will begin to learn more about Him and how He communicates with you. You will never have to ask yourself the question, "How do I know it's God?" because you have been in dialogue with Him and know how He leads you.

One important point to note about making this list and the process of praying overall is that it is quite the selfless act. I want you to bear this scripture in mind as you navigate this process: ***Psalm 37:4 - Delight thyself also in the Lord: and he shall give thee the desires of thine heart.*** Many Christian women approach marriage with the idea that it is solely for their physical needs to be met and it's all about what and who they want. This approach often leads women down the wrong path to the aisle. Marriage has little to do with you and everything to do with what God wants for you. What many miss is that, what God wants for you is ultimately what you want; it's the perspective that makes the difference. Now, the list has two components. It covers the areas of your future husband's life that you will be praying for, as well as the godly characteristics you need in a spouse. Instead of lamenting to God about what you want in a spouse and how soon you want it, try the selfless approach of committing the man you so desperately want to meet, to God in prayer.

The List Part One – Prayer Points

It is important to note the areas of focus for prayer. These prayer points will guide how you pray.

- Pray for his heart that it is lost in God
- Pray that he will be a God-lover
- Pray for his patience that he will wait and seek God for your hand.
- Pray that he is understanding
- Pray that he is someone who you can trust
- Pray about his loyalty and faithfulness to you and God
- Pray for his strength
- Pray for his protection

- Pray for the areas of intimacy
- Pray over the list of characteristics that you will write
- Pray for contentment
- Pray for commitment

The List Part Two – Godly Characteristics

This process made me realize something about myself that was too important a detail to miss. It made me realize that what I thought I needed in a man; let alone a husband was quite shallow. Good looks and materialistic items are good but they are not the most important characteristics this man should possess. God quickly revealed to me that godly traits focus more on the heart and characteristics of the man. My list was so long and detailed but believe me when I tell you that my husband is everything I need. For me, he had to be a good listener, he had to be creative and honour God. He also had to be set apart from the things of the world, funny, and charismatic. And, I had to accept the possibility that these godly traits may not appear in the imagined physical package.

When writing your list of godly characteristics, be prayerful and ask God to lead your hand. As you write, make note of what you see and prepare to look for these characteristics when potential suitors make their way to you.

Step Three – Time to Pray

This is the most interesting aspect of the journey in my opinion. Here is where it gets complex. Please be open. Understand that this is a sacred, and spiritual process. Pray in the spirit always. Allow God to give you the words from His heart. Don't be alarmed by some of the truths that may be uncovered. The process of praying for your future spouse requires much transparency with God. You must be able to face what you see and welcome the necessary changes you will need to make in your own life. Be open to the information that will be given to you through these prayers. You will receive clues and hints that will help you identify this spouse when he arrives. Handle your information with care. Note that it is not for everyone. Keep a journal if you must. Prayer is the information process that lets you know when to get ready and when to look up. This process requires faith and obedience. It requires selflessness and honour. Many see this as an easy process but it will STRETCH you and ensure that you're not only praying for but preparing for him as well.

NOTES

CHAPTER 7

The Counterfeit comes before the Real Deal

If you ask a wife or any married couple the question, "How is marriage?", you will hear that it is good, that it is beneficial, but it is challenging. I have yet to hear any seasoned married couple claim that marriage is a walk in the park. Yes, there are easy days and easy periods. There are even times when it is perfect. However, there are times when it seems as if all hell is breaking loose. Nothing worth having comes easy. And with marriage, it takes intention and discipline to ride the waves and get through its many seasons.

An important ingredient in having a solid, healthy marriage is having a solid, healthy spouse. By solid, I mean he is God's choice for you, you're compatible, there's chemistry, friendship and overall synergy. Having the right spouse who complements you and is equally yoked with you makes the journey a whole lot easier to navigate.

One thing to remember on this transition journey is that the enemy will always try to get you off track. He wants you to grow frustrated, he wants you to give up and ultimately, he wants you to marry wrong. Once you start praying and preparing your heart and mind for the big day, you have to start looking out for the counterfeit.

The counterfeit is a distraction sent to get you off track. He looks like what you want, sounds like what you want and every desire in your body will want to confirm that he is the one. Sadly, he pulls you away from God, distracts you from your purpose and completely wastes your time. If he doesn't add value to your life, he is probably sent to distract you. Don't even think for a second that the counterfeit is obvious or easy to identify. They are oftentimes men many women would consider noble men of God. They walk the walk and talk the talk but behind the façade they are no different than many of the men who are not in church.

Unfortunately, I have had a run in with a counterfeit and many of my friends have too. The story is the same across the board. After going through a period of prayer, preparation and receiving confirmation that marriage is on the way; someone appears who fits the bill. However, after entertaining the individual things struggle to match up to what God had promised. Immediately after realizing and letting go of the counterfeit, these women are aligned with the one who later becomes their husband. But how do you know if you're entangled with a counterfeit or how do you know what to look out for? There are a few tell-tale signs. Here are my observations:

He's Immature

There is a basic checklist to go through to determine if a man is fit for marriage.

- He is Making Future Plans. Men don't bring up things that they really would rather not talk about. ...
- You are Invited to Every Occasion. ...
- He is Punctual. ...
- There's an Increase in Touch. ...
- He Misses You. ...

- He Only Sees You. ...
- He Wants to Live Together. ...
- He Opens Up to You.
- The singles scene no longer appeals to him.
- He's financially independent.
- He's at least able to talk about the idea of commitment.
- He wants to be a father or is willing to be a step-father, if this applies to you.
- He's your boyfriend in name — your husband in spirit.

If a man is immature in any sense of the word it may mean he is not ready for such a huge commitment as marriage.

He's not so sure about you

If you have to constantly question how he feels about you then he is not the one for you. A man who is ready and serious about you will not leave you questioning or wondering about anything. He is direct, he is sure and he will communicate that without encouragement from you. Never put yourself in a position where you have to ask a man how he feels about you. Allow him to show you and if there are doubts or concerns address them and be prepared to walk away.

He doesn't pursue you

He is not sure about you so he doesn't pursue you. There is power and purpose in the pursuit. The pursuit is one thing that women should not compromise on. The pursuit communicates his intention clearly, it lets you know how much the pursuer values you and reveals his heart towards you. A man who does not pursue is not ready to maintain a marriage. The pursuit sets the foundation for trust and security. Men are known to go after the things that they want and value. When a godly man of integrity pursues, it shows that he knows what he wants and has made the necessary preparations to obtain what it is that he wants. He is on assignment from the Father to seek out and secure his wife. Never compromise or make excuses for a man who does not pursue you. Remember that your time and your attention are valuable. A man who does nothing to pursue you is not worth your time.

Pardon my language but he doesn't have his sh*t together

How is he going to marry you if he can't even provide for a date? On top of that, he has no true sense of self and identity. He is still a work in progress and it isn't your job to complete him. Many women have taken on the role of 'building a man'. While nothing is wrong with committing to growing **with** a man, that commitment should not be made at your expense. You both should complement each other and be in a position to help and nurture each other. If you find yourself taking care of him, spending all your money on him and the like, then you two are heading nowhere fast.

He's ready to compromise your purity

A man who respects you will honour your values and the way you carry yourself. The last thing a woman who is maintaining her purity needs is a man who has no respect for his own. One of the topics the bible is loud about is fornication and the importance of saving oneself for marriage. Sex and sexual acts are designed for marriage and as such we need to wait until marriage to indulge in those acts. A counterfeit will always push your boundaries of purity. If you find yourself struggling to maintain your purity in the presence of someone you think is ***the one***, then you may be entertaining your counterfeit.

When trying to identify whether or not you're entertaining your counterfeit, you can never go wrong with praying about it and seeking wise counsel from your trusted leaders. God will give you the answers that you need. If there is no ease, trust, favour, peace or clarity, then you may be setting yourself up to settle for your counterfeit. Don't let that be you.

NOTES

CHAPTER 8

The Definition of Wife

I've only been a wife for almost three years but one thing I've observed since being a Christian for seven years is how much young women and even older women covet the role of wife. Everyone admires the Pastor's wife and want to be the woman in that leadership position within the church. Being a young Christian entering into the church space, I too felt the pressure to get married and become a Pastor's wife. You see how the young girls fawn over the big hats and modest dresses and see how newly engaged couples are promoted to the upper echelons of the pews. I wanted that and all for the wrong reasons. I thought that step one in Christianity was to be baptized, step two was to be filled with the Holy Spirit and speak in tongues and step three was to get married. And boy was I on the lookout for Mr Right. That's how I ended up encountering Mr Counterfeit.

As funny as it may sound, it is a sad reality in our church spaces today. Not only is the pressure in local churches, it is also strong on social media. Instagram couples and influencers knowingly or unknowingly present marriage as the ultimate goal. The posts and stories add to the fanfare and fairy-tale and young girls around the world are hunting the right formula to obtain a ring.

Unfortunately, with that comes a myriad of definitions and examples of what it means to be a wife. And, as I have said earlier, God gives a blueprint but each blueprint is unique to the individuals it was created for. No two marriages will be the same and no two journeys to the altar will be the same. When you plug into one idea of marriage or what it means to be a wife, it's easy to become blindsided when reality hits. Placing your expectations solely on examples you see and hear around you is a sure recipe for disappointment.

Like the chapter on ***The Definition of Woman***, I've solicited a few perspectives from a few wives on what it means to be a wife.

Basillia Barnaby-Cuff
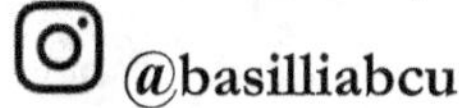
@basilliabcuff

"To me, being a wife means understanding that once I said *I do* 7 years ago, I am now one with my husband, and a part of my daily objective is ensuring the happiness, well-being, and overall contentment of my other whole. This means no longer looking at happiness from my perspective and doing things accordingly, but ensuring that I learn and apply his love language to my actions and words to yield best results where his happiness is concerned. That's a priority on my daily to do list.

Being his wife is understanding clearly that my husband and I are wired completely differently when it comes to our sexual nature, and that this sacred activity is of paramount importance to him. As such, I do my best to always fulfil his needs in that department with much excitement, adventure, spice and variety, not being afraid to be totally vulnerable to this man I call home.

Being a wife is respecting and honouring my husband at all times, in or out of his presence, and always seeking to protect his name. It's being fully cognizant that I'm with an imperfect human who makes mistakes, but who will always be on the receiving end of my support and solidarity. I will never join the crowd in tearing down his name, his character or disrespect him in any form. I will always seek to protect his honour.

As his wife, it is my innate duty to cover my husband physically and spiritually AT ALL TIMES, always encouraging, always pushing him to be the best version of himself, always supporting his goals and dreams no matter how far-fetched they may seem. I'm his number one cheerleader, and no matter what, I will always be in the front row with my pom poms and placards held high, shouting his name on the top of my voice. I am a mother, but I am always a wife first. It's not about putting him before my children, but being fully aware that in order to create a healthy and happy home for our children, we must first be healthy and happy ourselves. Being a wife has been one of my greatest blessings, and I wear this title with unequivocal pride and joy."

Andrea McCurdy

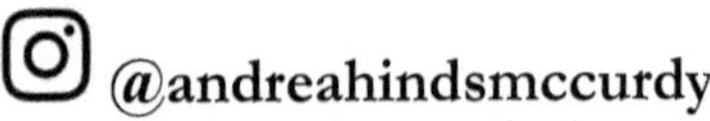

"Being a wife is so much more than wearing a ring, getting my surname changed, and having my friends be envious of my new found status. It is also so much more than having a legal sexual partner. Being a wife is understanding that I have been given the glorious opportunity to partner with someone in making a significant contribution not only to my immediate environment, (work, home life, etc.), but more importantly partnering with him in making a lasting impact on the world. It is important to me that my husband is a Christian who believes in the power of the Holy Spirit to change the world. It also means that I cannot be selfish with my own dreams and desires because whatever I do or not do impacts him and his effectiveness. It further means that I'm as much accountable to him as he is to me and in the same way that I want him to help me attain my goals, I should be present with him as he strives to make his own impact. It means that as he prayerfully watches over me, that I must do the same for him and speak the Word of the Lord over him at all times. It also means that I will challenge him, as he will challenge me to be better.

Finally, being a wife means that I am trustworthy and consistent and that I have earned and continue to earn my husband's trust so he can always find rest in my company and in my love for him. Being a wife means that I'm his loudest cheerleader, his harsh but fair critic and most importantly, his whole heart in stilettos."

Amoy Fearon

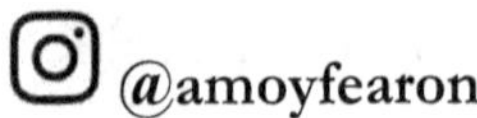

"Being a wife is a marvellous privilege and an experience like no other. To know that you have someone in your corner, your biggest cheerleader, to root for you, fight for you and to hold you. Someone you love, cherish, adore, respect and share all your secrets with. Your prayer partner, gym partner, lover, father of your children and best friend. A wife is one who showers her husband with unconditional love and support. Supporting his dreams and his desires. Being a wife can also be hard work. It requires selflessness, sacrifice, patience, forgiveness and unconditional love."

Datonya McLaren

"As I reflect on the word "wife" and what it means to me, I am brought back to a memory of my very first year of marriage. It was a summer when my church sister and I were travelling down to our church's national youth camp where we held a very engaging discussion on a number of topics. Exploring the topic of purpose and passion, she went on to ask me the question, "What are you passionate about?" Without hesitation, filled with great exuberance, I responded

"My husband! I am passionate about his growth. I am passionate about the man he will be and how God has asked me to partner with him in doing so." Many would say I merely spoke as a young and inexperienced wife, having no real understanding of what marriage truly entails, and to some extent, I do agree. Nevertheless, it has been all of 12 years and I am even more passionate about my husband. Was I passionate-every-single-day-of-every-single-year? A thousand times no, but I always knew in my heart - even in those stubborn, frustrating, and nerve-wracking moments - that as a wife, I was called to serve this man and partner with God to help him carry out his assignment here on earth. For as it is written, "for man was not made from woman, but woman from man. Neither was man created for woman, but woman for man." **1 Corinthians 11:8-9**

With that being said, I believe a wife is someone who chooses the path of marriage to serve another human being (her husband). Through engaging him to think, she stimulates his mind to surpass his limitations. She stimulates his spirit by covering him in prayer and reassuring him of God's promises for his life. She emphasizes the importance of him depending on God. She stimulates him sexually by making herself available and appealing so that she can fully satisfy his desires. As she works to maintain her external beauty, she is cognizant that her external beauty is fleeting and so she places greater emphasis on her inner beauty. This beauty is cultivated in her reverence and submission to her God as she lives out the words of Apostle Peter, "Do not let your adorning be external—the braiding of hair and the putting on of gold jewellery, or the clothing you wear— but let your adorning be the hidden person of the heart with the imperishable beauty of a gentle and quiet spirit, which in God's sight is very precious." **1 Peter 3.**

A wife is someone who communicates to her husband that she is his safe place, she is his friend and his prayer partner. She honours him in public places and private spaces and grasps that giving in, does not mean she is giving up or shutting down. She is comfortable trusting that when her words and efforts have failed, her prayers won't. The book of Proverbs confirms this when it states that the heart of her husband trusts in her, and he will have no lack of gain. She does him good, and not harm, all the days of her life. Have I always been this woman?

No, but the heart of a wife pants after these godly qualities and strives to be this and more to the one she serves."

NOTES

CHAPTER 9

The Transition

If you think waiting and preparing to meet your future spouse is hard then think again. Nothing beats the actual season of transition from Woman to Wife. That period after you've said yes to the ring and you're on your way with planning and preparing for the big day. It is in that time that you see hearts and true intentions revealed. The friends and family members you thought loved, supported you and had your back begin to show you that their commitment to you was baseless and all talk. My good friend and spiritual daughter, Natalya, said that weddings show you that the people who love you won't necessarily support you. That's a true and profound statement. How many of you think that love and support go hand in hand? It turns out that many love you enough to benefit from your proximity. They love what the closeness brings them but when it is time for them to pour out support for you it is a challenge for them. I've heard so many stories about the pre-wedding phase. This period will shake the foundation of every relationship you thought had depth. I have seen friendships end, families drift apart and individuals' selfishness, jealousy and hate come to the fore. When these things happen, don't be alarmed. It is God's way of purging your community before you enter into the sacredness of marriage. Because the truth is, you can't take everyone with you. You will need to be mindful of who you take counsel from and simply who knows your business when you become one with your spouse. It is a time for the two of you to become knitted together and only God needs to be included in that knitting. In **Ecclesiastes 4:12**, the Bible tells us that ***"though one may be overpowered, two can defend themselves. A cord of three strands is not quickly broken."*** It is necessary for the couples to learn to lean on each other and strengthen each other for the journey ahead, together.

Boundaries

In the transition period, you realise the need to set up boundaries. The purging of the community doesn't always mean that persons get cut off. It also means that you learn the importance of establishing and enforcing boundaries. A common misconception with boundaries in relationships is that they are only needed to ward off negative interactions or keep unnecessary contacts at bay. On the contrary, boundaries simply set the lines of respect in relationships. Boundaries can be described as how emotionally close you let people get to you. They are also where you draw the line within a relationship. They say how much you are willing to give or take before requiring that things change or deciding to call it quits. Friendships are usually challenged in the transition season. When you or a friend starts courting, the dynamic of the friendship changes significantly. The time that was once spent with you has now been divided so that the relationship between the newly found couple can blossom and grow into something beautiful. Depending on the maturity of the friend and the strength of the friendship, navigating this period can bring conflict and oftentimes separation. Setting boundaries early in the friendship can help to ease the discomfort in this season. Do not take it for granted that your friend will be understanding and should automatically fall in line with your life's changes. It is easier said than done for many, as we all process things differently and have varying outlooks on life. Whether you want to admit it or not, marriage affects the nature of platonic friendships. The effort that you put into preparing for marriage is sometimes needed to be applied to your meaningful platonic friendships to ensure that they make the transition with you.

Here are a few ideas on how to set some boundaries:

1. **Have an open and honest conversation.** In this conversation, highlight the importance of your relationship and where it is heading. Discuss the nature of your friendship and how things will change as time progresses. Try to understand your friend's needs and how best you can meet them given your current change in reality. A true friend will understand how important this transition is for you and adjust accordingly.

2. **Schedule time together.** Spending quality time together strengthens any meaningful relationship. Depending on your friendship dynamic, these meetings can be a simple phone call, video call or a

quick physical meet up. Whatever works best for the both of you, go for it.

3. **Keep your marital affairs private.** Your friend doesn't need to know the ins and outs of your marriage and neither should they feel comfortable enough to want to know. What happens between you and your spouse is just for the both of you. This can be an unspoken boundary. You simply do not entertain the conversations if and when they are brought up and you do not initiate. Your trust in your marriage is sacred and should be respected at all times.

You can't tell how your friendship or family dynamic will change but you can be prepared for whatever comes your way. With maturity, respect and the right conversations, those that aren't purged can be maintained and strengthened.

The Spiritual Warfare

If you truly want to get married, just know that you have to fight for it. The spiritual warfare that couples have to fight through during the transition phase is something that needs to be discussed more in the Christian spaces. The devil does not want you to get married. Pre-wedding warfare has nothing on

Murphy's Law. Whatever can go wrong will go wrong but it's the things you least expect. You can expect the craziest occurrences during this season. Your ex that you have not seen in over a decade may just make an appearance to profess his love for you. It could be as simple yet so frustrating as your bridesmaids' dresses somehow deliver as the wrong shade of green. Depending on how much your union will aggravate hell, you can expect individuals connected to your wedding to experience some level of personal warfare. Let's just say that a lot can happen and happen fast. You have to be prepared for anything.

There's one form of preparation that you absolutely cannot deny and that is prayer. Your spiritual tools should always be sharpened and ready for battle. You must remain in prayer and don't forget to include some fasting as well. Marriage is a covenant commitment that should not be entered into without spiritual readiness and awareness. Both you and your future spouse should be spiritually equipped to take on whatever comes your way.

I remember when I was getting ready to walk down the aisle, I went through one of the biggest character assassination attacks. There was one individual who felt the need to research my past, digging for dirt to present to my husband and his family. Luckily, the foundation of our union was being built on honesty and trust. There was nothing in my past that he wasn't aware of. The claims came but we were already united so the attempts were futile. That's just one example. I'm sure that if you ask the married couples around you, what their pre-wedding season was like, I bet they could share at least one instance where the devil showed his ugly head.

NOTES

CHAPTER 10

Marriage is a Mirror

When you stand in front of a mirror, what do you see? You see a reflection of yourself. That is, you staring back at you. I don't know if you notice but, in most mirrors, images are magnified. What you see appears larger and closer to you. I've heard many individuals refer to marriage as a mirror and I have had my own experience with this reality. I often say that I don't know a more refining, purifying and exposing experience. Marriage will truly humble you by causing you to see characteristics and qualities in yourself that you never thought existed.

It is important to be teachable though. Not only is it an admirable trait in life, but a necessary trait in marriage. You must be able to withstand criticism given in love. And, when received, there must be an interest in making the changes where necessary. Unfortunately, many don't believe in making such a compromise. They believe that once an individual expresses their love for another, they should be loved as they are for eternity. That is understandable but may I suggest to you that growth and evolution of any kind requires change. Change is an indicator of growth. Whatever doesn't change for the better becomes stagnant and stagnancy is never what we want in our marriage. When a body of water is stagnant it produces bacteria that causes an unbearable stench. Imagine your marriage wreaking of disappointment and failure because you or your spouse refused to grow or change?

As your marriage develops, various situations will occur that will challenge you, inspire you, or provoke you to wrath. For many, their natural reaction will shock them. It was easy to manage your emotions as a single woman. You knew that a soft answer would turn away wrath according to **Proverbs 15:1**. You know what the bible says and what your parents, pastors, mentors, or other spiritual figures have taught. You understand the implications of your words and the accompanying consequences yet, in a moment of rage, it all becomes a distant memory. In a split second, you are acting out of character then you are left face-to-face with a version of yourself you thought no longer existed.

If you are anything like me, you would try to justify it for a few minutes but a moment of ponder always leads me to the Father. He knows my heart more than anyone else. In that moment, He is the only one who can tell me I'm wrong and I am sober enough to receive it. And, truth is, if you have a relationship with the Holy Spirit, He will always tell you when you are wrong and guide you to the truth. I must admit that even correction from the Holy Spirit isn't easy to receive but with the right mind and attitude you will walk away with lessons unimaginable. Look at the bright side, the more time you spend with Him is the more refined you will become in speech and character.

Many women believe that marriage is all and only about the other person but are you bold enough or vulnerable enough to face yourself? Can you see the old you peeking through the cracks and not shun her but ask God to heal her? Can you be you, vulnerably? Can you give your soul to another human who has love so rich and tender, he is able to strip away every façade? Marriage exposes your true identity and who you are within shines forth with love, rarity and complexity. However, who that is, is completely up to you. Spend time with God working on your character. His love is safe, faithful, and true.

NOTES

CHAPTER 11

Whole Man; Whole Husband

(Contributed by JaQuan X. Gamble)

Wholeness is such an interesting discussion especially when it comes to men. Growing up, I personally did not hear conversations amongst men concerning what it means to be a "whole man" or how to be prepared for marriage, probably because the family construct has been in disarray, especially amongst the black diaspora. If we look back in history, we see black men being stripped from their manhood and their families which has created generational cycles of broken family structures and in turn, broken men.

Across cultures, manhood and understanding what it means to be a man can be quite confusing. I do not believe that this conversation concerning men and wholeness is one that has not been brought up in times past. I think it is becoming more of a necessity because of the liberation of women. Many women are coming to terms with their true identities and are no longer tolerating the toxic behaviours that men are possessing. Men's wholeness is a discussion that needs to be had in order for there to be a restoration of the family. Broken men produce broken family structures. When the family is broken, every other system connected to it will be as well.

Before we move forward, I believe it is vital to understand what it actually means to be whole. There are some common misconceptions of wholeness that are worth discussing. Being whole does not mean being "perfect" from the perspective of being without character flaw or the absence of struggle. Being whole does not mean that a man has arrived at anything to be prideful in. It also does not suggest that he will not make some mistakes in the future. Being whole means that a man understands his identity, and utilizes healthy strategies to be effective in every area of his life. For example, a whole man does not allow his emotions to govern his decisions nor does he allow other people's opinions to direct his decisions. A whole man does not disrespect his family even if his family is toxic. He is confident in who he is, what he does and what he has to offer. He also makes well thought-out decisions.

Wholeness is a result of a man who identifies areas of his character that are broken and need to be complete for the sake of his future. Aside from being healed for a woman, he should want to be whole because he wants to be a better man in his life. The interesting thing about healing is that it does not end. It is not something that you arrive at, but rather something you grow in daily. It is a continual process of perfecting and refinement that men will engage in for the rest of their lives. As time progresses, there are always areas in a man's life that need to be altered to be an even more productive man in the world. A whole man takes time to evaluate where he is emotionally, mentally, spiritually, financially and physically. In this evaluation, he investigates his strengths and weaknesses. It is almost as if he does a SWOT (strengths, weaknesses, opportunities and threats) analysis on his life. As a result, he makes the necessary changes by modifying his mindset and putting in place the necessary strategies for the sake of his future. This aspect requires a great deal of honesty, transparency and the willingness to adjust attitudes and behaviours. This is only a portion of it, though.

Typically, the behaviours that are seen are a result of the attitudes that are present in the heart and minds of men. Attitudes are created by a man's social context. How he behaves is indicative of the environment by which has groomed him to be the type of man he is. If a man wants to grow in his manhood, dimensions of his childhood must be confronted in order for him to be fruitful in the world, pre-wife. What reveals the level of wholeness a man has is his response to negative events, conflict or disagreements. Whatever coping mechanisms he utilizes in moments of great challenge are indicative of how whole he is. His responses will reveal everything about him.

Wholeness does not negate the frail nature of his humanity, but it does give you a reference point on what areas need development. A man will get upset. He will be frustrated. He will get hurt. He will have disappointments. He will have emotional moments. This is all part of human nature. How he responds to things of these events will allow himself and even his prospective spouse to understand what areas are still frail.

As stated before, manhood is complex. If you are a woman reading this book, you should know what to look for in a man worth settling down with. When engaging in this conversation, you must also understand that no man is perfect, but there are some things that are worth considering when dealing with someone you would want to spend the rest of your life with.

Principles of Manhood

One of the travesties of the world is that men are not taught to be men early enough. In history, we see that at the 12th or 13th birthday of a young man, he was at that point considered a man. Across cultures, there were celebrations commemorating his adulthood. The family and community knew that this young man is of age. This is the age of responsibility and good judgement becomes a primary organ in the infrastructure of one's manhood. We rarely hear stories in our 21st century culture like this.

It has always been my belief that men aren't developed properly. There is a level of arrested development that men have because they are not necessarily challenged in their manhood early on. This does not mean that they cannot enjoy their childhood and teenage years, but it does mean that parts of their character should be formed at this age. This is no one's fault. This is just the reality of our world today.

There are some key principles I believe that every man should adhere to pre-marriage:

Identity

As a man, your identity is the fundament to your existence. The stature of a man is strengthened by his identity. Identity is much deeper than just knowing who you are, but being confident in who you are and what you have to offer to the world. This does not mean a man should boast or be arrogant about himself. It just means that he does not allow anyone to undermine his position as a man. A man that is confident in his identity is not easily swayed by the opinions of other people.

A lot of times, men can develop their identity by what they do. They build their entire existence in their "doings," rather than just "being." At the moment, they lose everything, it is automatically a strike to their identity. They do not realize that what they do is only a by-product of who they are. They would not have the ability or the will to do what they do without their identity. A man's identity is not his ministry, his business endeavours, or anything else that is productive in nature. It is the reality of who he is. It is the man in private.

One of the ways you can tell the confidence of a man is how he responds in the presence of other men who are on his level. You can always tell the stability of his identity by how well he relates, connects with and interacts with other men. Men flourish in environments where there is both relatability and challenge because it proves how well he can withstand the pressures that are associated with being a man. Men challenge other men. **Proverbs 27:17** makes this clear by saying, "Iron sharpeneth iron; so, a man sharpeneth the countenance of his friend."

A man with a broken identity can be very toxic. Oftentimes, when a man has a broken identity, he tries to do and become like what he is connected to. He is like a chameleon and blends in whatever environment he is in. He has no clear sense of direction of his life. He also compares himself to people often and lives in an internal space of jealousy and envy. When a man has a broken identity, he may also have a superiority complex. He has a hard time honouring women, especially women who are more qualified or have more experience than he does. He believes that he is the end, all be all. He is highly misogynistic because of his brokenness.

A man who has identity issues generally has wounds from their mother or father. That is the origin of most identity crises in men. Men need affirmation. Let me say this again, men need affirmation, especially from their initial community which is their parents. This is not something that many men would actually confess, but this is the truth. Men need to feel valued and important as a youth. If one or both parents are absent, or if they are physically present and emotionally absent, that can leave a wound in their hearts. The presence of a parent is one of the most essential assets a boy can have through his growing years. If you ever see a man who is experiencing an identity crisis, a conversation should be had about his family context. Many adult men are just boys wrapped up in adult bodies because they have not matured in their identity as a man yet due to the wound of their parents.

A key part of a man's identity is his self-awareness. Self-awareness causes a man to be cognizant of himself internally and externally. It produces a consideration of his character, motives and emotions. He understands how to identify toxic behaviours from within himself that negatively affect other people and fix them. He makes sure that his character is intact before anything. He makes sure that he is walking in meekness, integrity, honour, wisdom, soundness and selflessness.

A man's character is highly important. It is almost a deal breaker. Women should evaluate a man's character before rushing into anything with him. His character will speak louder than anything. If he is rude, disrespectful, toxic, controlling, manipulative, indecisive, deceptive, secretive, misogynistic, overly promiscuous, violent, emotionless, apathetic, dangerous, aggressive, oppressive, entitled, unloving, unlovable, full of drama, or anything else that would cause unnecessary pain to you or your mental, emotional, physical or financial well-being, run!

The red flag is red and you do not need to settle for a trauma you can avoid. He will not be perfect of course, but you do not need to be put in a position of pain. That is not God's will for your life. You want someone who is honest, communicative, full of love, supportive, wise, integral, strong, but can be vulnerable, emotionally intelligent, a gentleman, graceful, masculine, humble, committed, respectful, faithful, has self-control, discerning, protective and more. His character matters! Do not be so infatuated with his nice looks and money that you miss the truth in his character.

One other aspect of a man's identity is his level of selflessness. Self-awareness causes a man to be discerning of himself. Selflessness causes a man to die to himself. Dying to himself does not mean that he loses himself, it means that he will put others before himself. In preparing for marriage, one of the first things that God spoke to me about was how much pride I still had in me. He was very clear that pride would be the demise to my future marriage. I began to intentionally put others before me. The epitome of a healed man is how selfless he is.

I tell people this all the time, Christ died for the church first. A man will lay everything down for the one he loves. I heard many men of successful marriages say that they would do anything to make sure their wife was good. Selflessness does not start in the dating process. It starts when he is alone and continues through marriage. Dying daily to self is necessary.

Love is sacrificial. Sacrifice requires selflessness. Selflessness addresses pride. A sign of a healed man is the fact that he does not allow for his pride to dictate how he treats the one he loves. Love is sacrificial. He will communicate through frustration. He will attempt to understand your emotions. He will make sure you feel safe even if it's uncomfortable for him. If there is anything that defines a whole man, it's selflessness. Selflessness governs his decisions and his dealings with every aspect of his life with his spouse or future spouse being top priority.

Purpose & Vision

A man should have a direction in his life. There is nothing more troubling than being a man without some sort of understanding of why you were put on this earth. A man without a purpose is a man without a vision. A man without a vision is a man without direction. A man without direction is a man that lacks productivity in life. Productivity yields impact. He does not have to be a multi-millionaire and living in a paid off house and have all of these materialistic expectations. He does not even have to be a Pastor or preacher for those women who are in ministry. He also does not have to have everything in his life together, but he should be actively engaged in what he was created to do and putting in the work to see greater in his life. He should be doing something substantial.

He should have evidence that he is positioning himself and his legacy for success. It is not the responsibility of a woman to raise a man. This does not mean that if you are with someone and they need help learning something new or healing in an area that you abandon them. This means that as a woman, you should not have to be his mother and his future spouse at the same time.

There are some things that should be in place in a man's life pre-marriage. One of those things is him being fruitful on the earth with a plan to reach the vision that he sees for himself. A man that is executing his plan is one that is committed to seeing results in his life.

I have heard many different love stories. I have heard stories about how the man and woman met in transitional periods in their life where one of them was freshly divorced or lost a job or something of that sort. I have heard stories where when they met neither one of them were ready for marriage and just decided to remain friends. I have also heard stories about the woman making more money than the man initially when they first met or even when they got married.

I said this to say that some of these situations are not always black and white. There are some grey areas. Give him grace to grow, but it is not your responsibility to grow him. The main concern about a prospective spouse is that you are sure that this is the one for you. Are you fully convinced? Is he actively pursuing his purpose? What is he bringing to the table? Does he have a table built? What is his vision? What is his plan to see the vision come to pass? What are his financial plans? What does he foresee for his family? What does he believe? What are some of his aspirations or dreams? How will he see them in reality? Do you believe in his ability to lead the house? What qualities of leadership does he exhibit? Can you trust that he can make decisions that will benefit your future together? When a man is positioned in purpose and pursuing vision, it proves a few things:

- He can be trusted to lead you somewhere
- He understands the value of his existence
- He recognizes that his life's mission is to serve
- He will see the fruit of his life

Stewardship is a word that we mainly use when we are talking about money. Stewardship is actually the management and multiplication of a thing. God instructed man to be fruitful, multiply, subdue the earth and have dominion. In other words, take what has been given to you and make more of it. Take care of what God has given you. When a man is in his purpose, his ability to take care of what he has dominion over is revealed. Whether he has children, a business, a career, a ministry, a home, a room in someone else's home, a car of any sort, his care for it should be something that you watch for. How well he manages these things will reveal to you how well he will manage your future marriage. You want someone who is a good steward over their life.

Emotional Intelligence

An aspect of manhood that is rarely discussed is the need for men to be emotionally intelligent and stable. The emotional wellbeing in men is something that brings a lot of scrutiny. Many people think men should not have feelings and if they do, it is deemed as feminine. It is believed that the main emotions that validate men's masculinity are anger and lust. This is a toxic thought pattern. Aggression does not equate to masculinity. Aggression does not make a man a man. His genitalia do not qualify his manhood either. Anger and lust should never lead a man. His emotions should never lead him at all.

Part of emotional intelligence comes from self-awareness that was aforementioned. Emotional intelligence is the ability for a person to identify, diagnose, control and express one's emotions in a healthy manner. Emotional intelligence is only revealed through interpersonal relationships. How a man is able to handle his non-romantic relationships is crucial to his maturity as a man. Society desires men to be aggressive, sex-driven, arrogant, homophobic, and domineering. This is not the peak of manhood. This is actually the breeding ground for creating sociopathic narcissists. The outcomes of conflict prove his character. Disagreement is the opportune time to evaluate a man's emotional intellect. If a man starts to get aggressive in disagreement, that is a red flag. If he responds to pressure by any means that are not healthy, that is something to be concerned about. If he is unwilling to apologize or confess his wrongs or change his behaviours, that is something to look for.

Most times, the lack of emotional intelligence in men is due to how society has taught parents to raise them. Telling a child they cannot cry is dangerous. Telling a young boy to suck it up and man up is toxic. Telling a young boy that crying is for girls is stupid. Telling him that he must be like a certain man that is portrayed on television is insensitive. Telling him that he is being like a girl or a sissy is a set up for homophobia and extreme perversion. Men are taught that women are objects. Men are taught that if you can't fight, you are "soft." They are taught that if you dress a certain way that is not "normal," they are feminine or gay.

These things that men are taught are the reason why men become abusive to women and children, are violent and full of hatred, and cannot love or be loved or stay faithful. Society has taught parents. These societal norms are the reason for gender trauma in men. There is a way to teach men to be masculine and not oppressive. An emotionally intelligent man can recognize what is or is not masculine and if it is a behaviour that is not profitable, they can adjust it. An emotionally intelligent man can be in the midst of conflict and instead of reacting in violence, they respond in grace and truth. An emotionally intelligent man knows how to communicate in the middle of frustration without becoming verbally abusive. He has strategies on how to deal with pain, grief and hurt.

He responds and does not react. Responses are everything. How a man responds is proof of the level of healing he has received. Men are trained to react. If something goes wrong, we react in whatever emotion is leading us in the moment. Men's reactions bring a lot of damage and sometimes that damage is irreversible. Men need to be healed just as much as society claims women do. How well a man responds to the negative event is indicative of how healed he is. I did not realize that I had rejection issues still until something that my fiancé did, triggered me. When she did this certain thing, I felt like I needed to isolate. It was not even something that was serious, but the first reaction I had was to isolate. I realized that I had an issue with rejection and abandonment. What I have realized is that some things that are triggers to us that other people do have nothing to do with them, but everything to do with us.

Sometimes, relationships end because men are too prideful to address what hurt them.

Emotional healing is necessary for a man to be an effective spouse. There are just some things that relationships do not have to go through. I am a believer in that. I have talked to countless married couples where they confess that they have had multiple conflicts, but there was never a time where divorce was an option. They would share how they avoided some of the traumas just in learning about the other person and knowing how to respond based upon how the other person receives. This is vital. One of the things men have to learn is that there is an authority on them by nature. If they are not healed, that authority could cause damage to a woman. When a man is whole, he understands how the woman he loves receives and speaks to her in a way she will receive it even if it is sensitive. He knows that if he is angry, to wait to speak. He knows not to yell at her. He knows that if he is frustrated, to take some time to respond. He knows when to give her space and let her think. Being a gentleman is not being a punk, it is being meek--having power under control.

Many men have a hard time being emotionally available due to childhood trauma. So many men are emotionally toxic and unstable because of the pains they never healed from in their youth. There are men whose fathers died prematurely. There are men who were adopted. There are men who were molested as a child by other men. There are men who were raised by all women. There are men who had a disability as a child. There are men who were exposed to pornography at three. There are men who were sex slaves. There are men who were starved as a child. There are men who did not grow up wealthy. There are men who were sheltered. There are men who watched their mother get beaten by their father. There are men who were rejected by their siblings. There are men who always had to fight competition. There are men whose fathers hated their presence. There are men who are attracted to men secretly and are afraid to tell someone. There are men who are feminine and are scared to do anything in public. There are men who cannot stop cheating if it killed them because they watched their father do it. There are men who have hidden pains that they need to address, but are afraid to feel. Men need to be healed from these things. A man that is willing to address these traumas and heal from them, is one that is worth keeping.

What if men who were in domestic violence situations knew how to be a man? What if men who molested women, other men, and children had an opportunity to talk about how they were molested as a child? What if men who got divorced could unpack the fact that he feels unloved by his wife due to his relationship with his mother which is why he cheated? What if men had an environment to address these issues pre-marriage? It is vital for men to be bold about getting the healing they need to become the man that is necessary in this world. The world does not need any more broken men leading it. The world needs healed and sober men. Women need healed men. A perfect man is Jesus, but a man who is following Him daily is one that will succeed in marriage. If there is anything to look for in a man is how well he can navigate emotional moments. Is he toxic? As a woman, you deserve to heal and a man that is healed as well. Do not settle because he has the look. If he is in his process, pray for him, but do not allow for your emotions to be entangled in anything that is not stable.

NOTES

CHAPTER 12

Whole Woman; Whole Wife

So, you're here. You think you're ready. You're eager to apply the nuggets you've learned so far in this book and start the journey from woman to wife. My one question for you is: are you whole? There has been an ongoing debate among Christian women on what is truly required for a woman to be considered ready for not only marriage but also ready to effectively navigate the world they occupy. The different generations seem to be at odds when it comes to this. It's the Boomer perspective vs the Millennial and GenZ perspectives. What's interesting about the debate is that even among the Millennials and GenZs there is a divide.

On one end, young women are advocating for womanhood to be the Suzie Homemaker/Martha Stewart type while on the other end, young women are advocating for Christian women to be strong, educated, liberal and independent.

When engaging women about their thoughts on womanhood, I realise that many don't know what to say or how to process their ideas. That suggests to me that they're not knowledgeable about the topic or they've never thought about it long enough to understand what womanhood means to them. When women are able to give a response, they usually reduce the definition to service or devotion to a man. They include motherhood, their ability to cook or tend to a house and their overall ability to serve. Their responses never include who they are as individuals, what they love, who they're called to be nor the value they bring to any table they sit at. It's always what they can do for others or how well they can suffer for a greater good.

While it is noble to be selfless and fulfil all the duties society has told us to be devoted to, you still need to have a sense of identity beyond what you can do to serve a man. Who are you? What makes you happy? When do you feel most centred? What do you like to do that makes you feel the most like yourself? What brings you joy and satisfaction? How do you wish to leave your mark in this world? What assignment has God given you to fulfil while you're here? You need to connect with God and grow in your identity and purpose in Him as an individual before you can begin to pour into others.

Can we pause for little heart to heart?

My heart aches for young women who were raised seeing their mothers, aunts, sisters and grandmothers suffer for the betterment of their families. To see strong women put themselves last, make sacrifices and neglect their well-being for the sake of 'keeping the family together', breaks by heart. The trauma that women have witnessed have subconsciously shaped the way they view womanhood and the function of a woman in her family. In trying to set the record straight and heal the breakdown in our lineage, many have dressed the same problems in new clothes in an attempt to be the change they want to see. Women want to live better marital lives. They want long, healthy, wholesome marriages; but to get there they continue to run in circles. Why? Because the women who have successfully or seemingly made it to the altar fail to present the God-view on womanhood and what I like to call 'wifery'. This book is here to help you grasp a sense of reality while taking the necessary steps to be ready at the altar. You don't have to know how to bake a cake, clean an entire house, become a sex doll for your husband or have the desire to pop ten children out to be ready. What you need is a submitted heart to God, a relationship with Him and the desire to have him shape your life according to His plans for you. He will fit the pieces together and prepare you for the life ahead. Don't be surprised if your process breaks the status quo. Some will be stay at home mothers who serve their husbands and share Christian influencer content on Instagram. While, others will be leading women in the workplace, political spaces and the marketplace. All while building strong, healthy, Christian families along with their spouses who love them unconditionally. Whatever your womanhood looks like as you develop and grow in God, will be the perfect foundation for who you are as a wife. Remember, all our journeys are different. We aren't all called to be the same type of woman. However, what you will be is a woman after God's own heart whose submission and service to her family flows through Him.

Your mental health, self-awareness and emotional well-being are just three pillars that strengthen the entire make-up of the woman. So, I ask again, are you whole? Spend some time working on you. Take that class, go to therapy, work on improving your image and being the best version of you. It takes more than domestic skills and sexual prowess to maintain a strong, healthy marriage. What you bring to the table also matters. The more filled you are, the more you're able to pour into your family. And the same goes for the man you choose to marry. What he brings to the table also matters. I pray you become whole so that you will be able to identify and flourish in wholeness when it comes.

NOTES

www.ingramcontent.com/pod-product-compliance
Lightning Source LLC
LaVergne TN
LVHW010109170826
845678LV00012B/2311

* 9 7 8 9 7 6 9 6 3 9 8 8 1 *